Bible Quizzles and Quotes

Based on the *New International Version* of the Bible

by Fannie L. Houck

STANDARD PUBLISHING
Cincinnati, Ohio

All Scripture quotations in this publication are from the
Holy Bible, New International Version.
Copyright © 1973, 1978, 1984 International Bible Society.
Used by permission of Zondervan Bible Publishers.

ISBN 0-87403-676-3

Copyright © 1992,
The STANDARD PUBLISHING Company, Cincinnati, Ohio.
Division of STANDEX INTERNATIONAL Corporation.
Printed in U.S.A.

Permission is granted to purchaser of book
to reproduce pages for classroom use only—not for resale.

Contents

Adam and Eve 5
What Animal Am I? 6
Beasts Unique 7
Believe It or Not! 8
Which Bible Woman Am I? 9
Bible People Ladder 11
Bible Firsts 12
Baby Moses and Baby Jesus Mix-Up 13
Books: Old or New? 14
Come-On-In and Counsel CryptoQuote 15
Double Trouble 16
Faith and Fire Categories 17
A Family Ladder 18
What Food Am I? 19
From the Heart and Isaiah's Praise Cryptogram 20
Genesis Firsts 21
How Many? 22
Jairus' Story 23
The Master Healer 24
Mercy Child Categories 25

Middle Verse and How Far?	26
Women: Old or New?	27
Naaman's Problem	28
Men: Old or New	29
Older or Younger?	30
Patience Pays and A Sure Guard	31
Quote Anagrams	32
Sons of Jacob Ladder	33
Still More Quote Anagrams	34
Triumphal Entry	35
True or False?	36
Twelves	37
Who Would You Rather Be?	38
Who Are We?	39
Liars	40
Who Said It?	41
Who, What, How?	42
Whose Relatives?	43
Decipher the Speaker	44
Answers	46

Adam and Eve

1. Adam's job was to take care of a beautiful _____.

2. Adam and Eve could eat from every tree in the garden except _____.

3. _____ named all the beasts and birds.

4. God removed a rib while Adam was _____.

5. Until they sinned, Adam and Eve felt no _____.

6. Adam was created from _____.

7. Eve was created from _____.

8. My mate named me. Who am I? _____.

9. A crafty serpent deceived _____.

10. After they sinned, what two things kept Adam and Eve from eating from the tree of life again? _____ and _____.

11. God created Adam and Eve on the _____ day.

12. Adam and Eve had sons named _____, _____, and _____.

(1) Genesis 2:15; (2) Genesis 2:16-17; (3) Genesis 2:19; (4) Genesis 2:21; (5) Genesis 2:25; (6) Genesis 2:7; (7) Genesis 2:21, 22; (8) Genesis 3:20; (9) Genesis 3:1-6; (10) Genesis 3:24; (11) Genesis 1: 26-31; (12) Genesis 4:25

1992, The STANDARD PUBLISHING Company
Permission is granted to reproduce this page for classroom use only—not for resale

What Animal Am I?

1. We mauled forty-two youths who mocked Elisha. _____

2. Jonah spent three days inside me. _____

3. While Moses was away, Aaron melted jewelry and made me for people to worship. _____

4. Unhurt, Paul shook me off into the fire after I bit him. _____

5. My skin fooled Isaac into thinking that Jacob was Esau. _____

6. A wise man advised people to study me and learn from me. _____

7. Daniel spent a night in our den but we didn't harm him. _____

8. The man hired to feed us was so hungry he wanted to eat our food. _____

9. Samson killed a thousand Philistines with my jawbone. _____

10. During a famine, we carried food to Elijah. _____

11. As the Jews rebuilt the wall around Jerusalem, an Ammonite said that if I climbed on it I'd break it down. _____

(1) 2 Kings 2:23, 24; (2) Matthew 12:40; (3) Exodus 32:1-4 (4) Acts 28:3; (5) Genesis 27:15-29; (6) Proverbs 6:6; (7) Daniel 6:19-22; (8) Luke 15:16; (9) Judges 15:15, 16; (10) 1 Kings 17:6; (11) Nehemiah 4:3

Beasts Unique

God created many unique and interesting creatures. Can you draw a line from each animal to its clue?

1. I'm the biggest land animal. blue whale

2. I'm the biggest animal of all, up to 95 feet long. ostrich

3. My tongue is about as long as my body. centipede

4. I live the longest, maybe over 100 years. chameleon

5. I'm the smallest bird, as short as two inches. giant tortoise

6. I'm an egg-laying mammal. giraffe

7. I'm the fastest running bird. I can run 35-50 miles per hour. elephant

8. I have as many as 340 legs. horse

9. I'm the land animal with the largest eyes. hummingbird

10. I've got the longest neck. platypus

Believe It or Not!   Who Am I?

1. During my only son's funeral, Jesus brought him back to life. _____

2. Jesus cured my blindness. _____

3. Jesus drove the evil spirit out of me and into a nearby herd of pigs. _____

4. When Jesus called me out of the grave, I'd been there for four days. _____

5. In twelve years no doctor had helped me, but when I touched Jesus' cloak He healed me instantly. _____

6. My father, a ruler of a synagogue, asked Jesus to come heal me. He did. _____

7. Jesus cured ten men who had the same disease. I alone returned to thank Him. _____

8. A poisonous snake bit me, but I was not harmed. _____

9. I rose from the dead and brought great joy and comfort to my followers. _____

10. I was taken up into heaven in a whirlwind. _____

(1) Luke 7:11-15; (2) Mark 10:46-52; (3) Mark 5:1-13; (4) John 11:1-38; (5) Luke 8:43-48; (6) Luke 8:41-42; (7) Luke 17:12-16; (8) Acts 28:3-5; (9) John 20:15, 20; (10) 2 Kings 2:11

© 1992, The STANDARD PUBLISHING Company
Permission is granted to reproduce this page for classroom use only—not for resale

Which Bible Woman Am I?

Remove each woman's disguise by unscrambling her name.

1. I laughed when the Lord said I, an old woman, would have a baby.

    A SHAR　　＿＿＿＿＿＿＿＿＿＿＿＿＿

2. I liked to sit and listen to Jesus.

    ARMY　　＿＿＿＿＿＿＿＿＿＿＿＿＿

3. I married a man who could have become a pharaoh.

    HARP POIZ　　＿＿＿＿＿＿＿＿＿＿＿＿＿

4. I provided clothing for widows and orphans.

    SOD CAR　　＿＿＿＿＿＿＿＿＿＿＿＿＿

5. I returned to Moab instead of going with Naomi to her country.

    RO APH　　＿＿＿＿＿＿＿＿＿＿＿＿＿

6. I hid spies on my rooftop and later became the mother of Boaz.

    BAR HA　　＿＿＿＿＿＿＿＿＿＿＿＿＿

© 1992, The STANDARD PUBLISHING Company
Permission is granted to reproduce this page for classroom use only—not for resale.

7. Both my husband, David, and my son Solomon were kings of Israel.

   BHAH BEATS _____

8. I am an orphan and queen who saved my people.

   HE REST _____

9. I watered a stranger's camels and soon went with him to marry a man I had never met.

   RAKE HEB _____

10. My husband Ahab and I are famous for being very wicked.

    ZEEL JEB _____

11. A book of the Bible is named for my grandson. His mother's name is NIC UEE. _____ Mine is SOLI. _____

12. My son lived in the wilderness.

    BEZIL ATEH _____

(1) Genesis 18:12; (2) Luke 10:39; (3) Exodus 18:2; (4) Acts 9:36, 39; (5) Ruth 1:14; (6) Joshua 2:1-6, Matthew 1:5; (7) 2 Samuel 12:24; (8) Esther 2:7, 8:3-8; (9) Genesis 24:45, 46, 57-67; (10) 1 Kings 16:30, 31; (11) 2 Timothy 1:5; (12) Luke 1:57, 80

Bible People Ladder

Each missing word names a Bible person and a Bible book. Each blank stands for one letter of the word.

1. Few have troubles as bad as mine.   _ _ B
2. I am a major prophet.   _ _ _ I _ _
3. My tiny book is just before Jonah.   _ B _ _ _ _ _
4. I wrote Acts, and one of the gospels.   L _ _ _
5. In vision I saw wheels and dry bones.   _ _ E _ _ _ _

6. Briefly, I walked on water.   P _ _ _ _
7. Hungry lions kept me company.   _ _ _ _ E _
8. I took Jesus' mother into my home.   _ O _ _
9. Paul wrote to me about Onesimus.   P _ _ _ _ _ _ _
10. I am second of the minor prophets.   _ _ _ L
11. I won an important beauty contest.   E _ _ _ _ _

Bible Firsts

1. Israel's first king   _____

2. Jesus' first miracle   _____

3. First Gentile to become a Christian   _____

4. First book of the Bible   _____

5. Winner of the first beauty contest   _____

6. First Christian martyr   _____

7. First four words of the Bible   _____

8. First foreign missionaries   _____

9. First parable in New Testament   _____

10. First beatitude   _____

11. First of the ten plagues in Egypt   _____

12. First disciples called by Jesus   _____

13. First haircut story   _____

14. First verse of Psalm 23   _____

15. First book of the New Testament   _____

16. First hunter mentioned in the Bible   _____

17. First color named   _____

18. First sword mentioned in the Bible   _____

19. First New Testament prayer instruction   _____

20. Man who built the first altar   _____

(1) 1 Samuel 9:17; (2) John 2:1-11; (3) Acts 10; (5) Esther 2; (6)Acts 7:59, 60 (7) Genesis 1:1; (8) Acts 13; (9) Matthew 13:3; (10) Matthew 5:3; (11) Exodus 7:14-18; (12) Matthew 4:18; (13) Judges 16:19; (16) Genesis 10:9; (17) Genesis 1:30; (18) Genesis 3:24; (19) Matthew 5:44; (20) Genesis 8:20

Baby Moses Mix-Up

Exodus 1:22; 2:1-10

Put the story in order by numbering its parts 1-5.

_____ Jochebed prepares a special basket

_____ Miriam watches to see what happens

_____ Pharaoh orders all Hebrew boy babies killed

_____ Pharaoh's daughter finds a beautiful baby

_____ Jochebed puts Moses and the basket in the river

Baby Jesus Mix-Up

Luke 2:2-20

Put the story in order by numbering its parts 1-5.

_____ Shepherds see the baby

_____ Angels announce the baby's birth

_____ Joseph and Mary go to Bethlehem

_____ The shepherds tell others the good news

_____ Jesus is born

Books: Old or New?

Where will you find each of the following books of the Bible? In the Old or New Testament?

1. Chronicles _____
2. Corinthians _____
3. Ephesians _____
4. Genesis _____
5. Hebrews _____
6. Isaiah _____
7. Judges _____
8. Luke _____
9. Malachi _____
10. Matthew _____
11. Obadiah _____
12. Proverbs _____
13. Psalms _____
14. Revelation _____
15. Romans _____
16. Timothy _____

© 1992, The STANDARD PUBLISHING Company
Permission is granted to reproduce this page for classroom use only—not for resale

Come-On-In CryptoQuote

Solve this cryptogram by reading every other letter in each word group. Start with the first letter.

IA AEMB TTHQEV GEACTDEH; WDHOOREOVBEYRG EBNETCEIRASF TNHAREOYUYGTHQ MEEC WRIHLVLE BJEE SSAWVAEVDZ. HAEN WEICLDLH CAOEMNEY IGNR AONWDH GDOY OWUTTF, AQNFDE FNIANNDY PSAESSTQUFRREL.

JLOEHCNP 1203:94

Counsel CryptoQuote

Solve this cryptogram by reading every other letter. Start with the second letter of each word group.

NDYO OWUHTAST TIHS ERAIHGDHGT SAONCD SGUOHOYD LIKN CTIHLE ELEOGRWDHS DSOIHGTHAT, WSDO NTOHTAGT OIST TMPAIY JGTO EWHEALNL AWRIHTLH RYFOWU.

SDREWUTTMENRBOVNCOXMZY 56:3128.

© 1992, The STANDARD PUBLISHING Company
Permission is granted to reproduce this page for classroom use only—not for resale

Double Trouble

Which two Bible characters could make the statements below?

1. We obeyed God and took a three-day trip to offer a sacrifice. God sent a ram. _____ _____

2. The younger of us brothers managed to get the birthright blessing. _____ _____

3. I knocked a warrior down with a stone, then killed him with his own sword. _____ _____

4. People still talk about our close friendship _____ _____

5. God struck us both dead after we lied about the sale price of some property. _____ _____

6. We had a part in the first murder. _____ _____

7. We are cousins and evangelists. The older baptized the younger. _____ _____

8. An angel told us to flee to Egypt to protect our young child. _____ _____

9. Jesus liked to visit us and our brother in our home in Bethany. _____ _____

10. We were banished from the Garden of Eden. _____ _____

(1) Genesis 22:3, 13; (2) Genesis 27:30-32; (3) 1 Samuel 17:23, 48-51; (4) 1 Samuel 18:1; (5) Acts 5:1-10; (6) Genesis 4:8; (7) Matthew 3:13-15; (8) Matthew 2:13; (9) John 11:1-2; (10) Genesis 1:26; Genesis 3:20-24

Faith and Fire Categories

In each box, write one or more words that fit the category given above it. Start the words with the letter given at the left.

	Bird	Body Part	Bible Word
F			
A			
I			
T			
H			

	Bible Event	Bible Object or Animal	Something that Moves
F			
I			
R			
E			

A Family Ladder

1. I am Reuel's daughter. My father's other name is Jethro. __ I __ __ __ __ __

2. I am Tubal-Cain's sister. N __ __ __ __

3. I'm the daughter of Abihail. My cousin adopted me. __ __ T __ __ __

4. I'm Laban's younger daughter. __ __ __ H __ __

5. Bethuel's my dad. I had twins. __ __ __ E __ __ __

6. I am Drusilla's husband F __ __ __ __

7. I'm Phanuel's daughter, and a prophetess. A __ __ __

8. I'm the daughter of Amram, who was a slave in Egypt. M __ __ __ __

9. I'm King Saul's younger daughter. __ I __ __ __ __

10. My father tricked Jacob into marrying me. L __ __ __

11. When Jesus visited, I didn't help my sister. __ __ Y

(1) Exodus 2:18-21; (2) Genesis 4:22; (3) Esther 2:15; (4) Genesis 29:16; (5) Genesis 22:23, 25:21-24; (6) Acts 24:24; (7) Luke 2:36; (8) Numbers 26:59; (9) 1 Samuel 14:49; (10) Genesis 29:20-23; (11) Luke 10:38-40

© 1992, The STANDARD PUBLISHING Company
Permission is granted to reproduce this page for classroom use only—not for resale

What Food Am I?

1. Abigail sent two hundred cakes of me as a gift to David and his warriors. _____

2. Esau traded his birthright to his brother for me. _____

3. Two of the twelve spies carried a cluster of me back from the promised land on a pole. _____

4. Samson ate some of me that he found in the carcass of a dead lion _____

5. While traveling in the wilderness the Israelites got hungry for these strong-flavored foods. _____

6. A woman of Canaan reminded Jesus that dogs eat me when I fall from the table. _____

7. I grow on trees and am pressed to make oil. _____

8. At Jesus' command, servants filled jars with water and then poured me out. _____

9. God's people ate me for forty years while they wandered in the wilderness. _____

10. When a boy shared me with Jesus, He fed a crowd. _____

1) 1 Samuel 25:18-20; (2) Genesis 25:30-34; (3) Numbers 13:23; (4) Judges 14:8, 9; (5) Numbers 11:5; (6) Matthew 15:27; (7) Micah 6:15; (8) John 2:6-10; (9) Exodus 16:35; (10) John 6:9-13

© 1992, The STANDARD PUBLISHING Company
Permission is granted to reproduce this page for classroom use only—not for resale

From the Heart

Discover the message of the heart by reading every other letter in each word group. Start with the second letter.

EI RWPIWLIL SPARBAAICSQE HYTOEU, DO CLMODRLD,

RWFIJTTH YAMLGL BMWY EHLEEANRAT; OI LWSIQLWL

ATFETLBL GOCF TAJLBL TYIODUTR

GWMOZNQDREARSS.

RPESWAQLAM 79:41

Isaiah's Praise

Find out what Isaiah said by reading every other letter of this cryptogram. Start with the first letter.

ON LVOPRRDO, YXOYUB AARCED MGYJ GNORDD; IS

WTIZLALH EFXEAALLTV YTOWUM ALNXDL

PBRCAEIFSDEG YNOPUMRL NHATMYED, FROQRE IRNS

PHEORAFZEDCXTO FVAEIXTWHQFOURLTNMEPSXSS

YTOHUV HVARVSEU DIOSNCEC

MWANROVPENLDORUFSS TVHHIANWGZSZ,

TAHSIDNFGTSR PLLKAJNHNGEFDS LAOQNWGE

ARGTOY.

IDSFAGIHAJHK 2153:13

Genesis Firsts

1. First lie _____
2. First baby _____
3. First curse _____
4. First clothing _____
5. First operation _____
6. First boat builder _____
7. First global disaster _____
8. First son of Abraham _____
9. First human who didn't die _____
10. First offerings mentioned _____
11. First recorded command _____
12. First recorded dream _____
13. First known twins _____
14. First son of Jacob _____
15. First human sin _____
16. First murderer _____
17. First grandson _____
18. First couple _____
19. First death _____
20. First home _____

All in Genesis) (1) 3:4; (2) 4:1; (3) 3:14; (4) 3:7; (5) 2:21; (6) 6:13, 14; (7) 7:17-21; (8) 16:15; (9) 5:24; (10) 4:3, 4; (11) 1:28; (12) 20:3; (13) 25:24-26; (14) 35:23; (15) 3:6; (16) 4:8; (17) 4:17; (18) 3:20; (19) 3:21; (20) 2:8;

© 1992, The STANDARD PUBLISHING Company
Permission is granted to reproduce this page for classroom use only—not for resale

How Many?

1. ... sons did Jacob have? _____

2. ... years did Moses live? _____

3. ... disciples did Christ call? _____

4. ... years did Methuselah live? _____

5. ... brothers did Benjamin have? _____

6. ... how many wives did Jacob have? _____

7. ... people were saved in Noah's ark? _____

8. ... feet tall was Goliath the Philistine? _____

9. ... feet long and wide was Noah's ark? _____

10. ... years older than Moses was Aaron? _____

11. ... years old was Noah when the flood came? _____

12. ... days and nights did it rain during the flood? _____

13. ... women brought spices to anoint Jesus' body? _____

14. ... commandments did God write on tables of stone? _____

15. ... brother and sisters did the prophet Samuel have? _____

16. ... years did Jacob work to obtain Rachel as his wife? _____

17. ... years old was Jesus when He began His public ministry? _____

(1) Genesis 35:22; (2) Deuteronomy 34:7; (3) Luke 6:13; (4) Genesis 5:27; (5) Genesis 35:22; (6) Genesis 35:23-26; (7) 1 Peter 3:20; (8) 1 Samuel 17:4; (9) Genesis 6:15; (10) Exodus 7:7; (11) Genesis 7:6; (12) Genesis 7:12; (13) Mark 16:1; (14) Deuteronomy 4:13; (15) 1 Samuel 2:21; (16) Genesis 29:18-28; (17) Luke 3:23;

Jairus' Story

Choose the correct ending.
If you need help, check Matthew 9:18-26.

1. Jairus was a
    A. tax man   B. merchant   C. ruler

2. His much-loved
    A. daughter   B. cousin   C. wife

3. had just
    A. moved.   B. died.   C. married.

4. Jairus said to Jesus, "Come touch her with your
    A. hand."   B. staff."   C. robe."

5. Jesus went to Jairus'
    A. workshop   B. house   C. rooftop

6. and told the crowd to
    A. be quiet.   B. come inside.   C. go away.

7. He said, "The girl is not dead but is
    A. asleep."   B. playing."   C. pretending."

8. The crowd
    A. stoned Him.   B. believed Him.   C. laughed at Him.

9. Jesus took the girl's
    A. hand   B. temperature   C. comb

10. and she
    A. screamed.   B. got up.   C. rolled over.

11. Soon everyone heard her
    A. terrible cough. B. sad song.   C. wonderful story.

The Master Healer

Jesus healed these human miseries, mentioned in Matthew 4:24; 8:14, 15; and 11:5. Write your answers on the blanks that follow each clue. Put one letter on each blank.

1. Lifeless condition   _ _ _ **D**
2. Discomfort   _ _ **I** _
3. A skin disease   _ _ _ _ _ **S** _
4. High body temperature   _ _ _ **E** _
5. Those unable to walk   _ _ _ **A** _ _ _ _ _
6. Demon-   _ _ _ _ **S** _ _ _
7. Unable to hear   _ **E** _ _
8. Unwell   **S** _ _ _

Mercy Child

In each box, write one or more words that fit the category given above it. Start the words with the letter given at the left.

	Mineral	Animal	Cooked Food
M			
E			
R			
C			
Y			

	Body Part	Bible Person	Finger Food
C			
H			
I			
L			
D			

Middle Verse

Cross out every M, except when two M's are side-by-side (leave one). Then read the Bible's middle verse.

IMTM IMSM BMEMTMTMEMRM TMOM TMAMKMEN

RMEMFMUMGMEM IMNM TMHMEM LMOMRMDM

TMHMAMNM TMOM TMRMUMSMTM IMNM MMAMNM.

PMSMAMLMM 1M1M8M:8M

How Far?

How far will Jesus move our sin away from us? To find out, cross out all the XXs in this Bible verse.

AXSX FXAXRX AXSX TXHXEX EXAXSXTX IXSX

FXRXOXMX TXHXEX WXEXSXTX, SXOX FXAXRX

HXAXSX HXEX RXEXMXOXVXEXDX OXUXRX

TXRXAXNXSXGXRXEXSXSXIXOXNXSX FXRXOXMX UXSX.

PXSXAXLXMX 1XOX3X:1X2X

Women: Old or New?

Identify each of these women and tell which part of the Bible (Old or New Testament) contains her story.

1. Abigail _____
2. Anna _____
3. Deborah _____
4. Dorcas _____
5. Elizabeth _____
6. Esther _____
7. Lydia _____
8. Martha _____
9. Mary Magdalene _____
10. Miriam _____
11. Naomi _____
12. Rahab _____
13. Ruth _____
14. Salome _____
15. Sapphira _____
16. Zipporah _____

© 1992, The Standard Publishing Company
Permission is granted to reproduce this page for classroom use only—not for resale

Naaman's Problem

Choose the correct ending to each statement.
For help, check 2 Kings 5:1-16.

1. Naaman had
    - A. boils.
    - B. leprosy.
    - C. a broken leg.

2. From a slave girl he heard about a
    - A. priest
    - B. king
    - C. prophet

3. in Samaria who could
    - A. cure him.
    - B. hide him.
    - C. advise him.

4. The king of Israel tore his robes because he could not
    - A. see Naaman.
    - B. heal Naaman.
    - C. hear Naaman.

5. Then Naaman went to Elisha, who told him to
    - A. jump
    - B. lie down
    - C. wash himself

6. in the Jordan River
    - A. five times.
    - B. seven times.
    - C. six times.

7. Naaman refused because the Jordan wasn't
    - A. clean enough.
    - B. deep enough.
    - C. good enough.

8. His servants talked him into going back and
    - A. apologizing.
    - B. eating.
    - C. bathing.

9. After Naaman did as Elisha said, he lost his
    - A. appetite.
    - B. spots.
    - C. energy.

10. Naaman offered Elisha a gift, and Elisha
    - A. refused.
    - B. accepted.
    - C. gave him a mule.

11. Naaman said, There's no God in all the world except in
    - A. Israel.
    - B. Egypt.
    - C. Moab.

© 1992, The Standard Publishing Company
Permission is granted to reproduce this page for classroom use only—not for resale

Men: Old or New?

Identify each man and tell whether his story is in the Old or New Testament.

1. Abel _____
2. Absalom _____
3. Agrippa _____
4. Enoch _____
5. Eutychus _____
6. Jairus _____
7. Jonathan _____
8. Joseph _____
9. Josiah _____
10. Judas Iscariot _____
11. Lazarus _____
12. Mephibosheth _____
13. Pontius Pilate _____
14. Zacchaeus _____

© 1992, The Standard Publishing Company
Permission is granted to reproduce this page for classroom use only—not for resale

Older or Younger?

In each of the following pairs, who was born first?
Tell why you think so.

1. Cain and Abel   _____

2. Joseph and Benjamin   _____

3. Elijah and Elisha   _____

4. David and Goliath   _____

5. Solomon and Absalom   _____

6. Jesus and John the Baptist   _____

7. Abraham and Lot   _____

8. Moses and Joshua   _____

9. Adam and Eve   _____

10. Abraham and Sarah   _____

11. Leah and Rachel   _____

12. Miriam and Jochebed   _____

13. Ruth and Naomi   _____

14. Saul and Jonathan   _____

15. David and Jesse   _____

16. John the Baptist and Zechariah   _____

17. Hannah and Samuel   _____

18. Methuselah and Enoch   _____

19. Moses and Aaron   _____

(1) Genesis 4:1, 2; (2) Genesis 35:24, 30:24, 35:18; (3) 2 Kings 2:11, 12; (4) 1 Samuel 17:33; (5) 1 Chronicles 3:1-5; (6) Luke 1:13, 24-31; (7) Genesis 11:27 (8) Exodus 2; Deuteronomy 34:7, Joshua 23:1, 24:29; (9) Genesis 2:22; (10) Genesis 17:17; (11) Genesis 29:16; (12) Numbers 26:59; (13) Ruth 1:4, 8, 12 (14) 1 Samuel 13:16; (15) Matthew 1:6; (16) Luke 1:13; (17) 1 Samuel 1:20 (18) Genesis 5:21; (19) Exodus 7:7

© 1992, The Standard Publishing Company
Permission is granted to reproduce this page for classroom use only—not for resale

Patience Pays

Solve this cryptogram by reading every other letter, starting with the first one in each word group.

BHEETBTEEDRW AW PHALTOINEINPTS MSARNL

TOHSAWNH AI WAAXRNREIGORRE, AR MIAZNS

WDHSOE CEOVNTTORTOMLESY HFIASF

TTECMHPAEERG TMHRAINN OHNVEI WZHSOB

TSAPKFEJSI AH CEIXTIYN.

PGROOLVAECRBBNS 1263:3425

A Sure Guard

Start with the first letter in each group and read every other one to find out who is watching over you.

HTEV WFIELBLR CSOXMHMFAANIDL HTINSJ

AONDGEEBLWSL CTOVNGCHEFRBNEIBNOGU YPOYUM

TMOO GRUHAFREDR YWOCUW IXNA

AQLGLSYROEUWRT WHAGYFSD.

PGSIAVLEMD 9210:1215

© 1992, The STANDARD PUBLISHING Company
Permission is granted to reproduce this page for classroom use only—not for resale

Quote Anagrams

To complete each Bible verse, unscramble the numbered words and write them in the second column. Then write the words on the corresponding, numbered blanks.

A1. aeiimtt		Do not (1)_____ what is evil
A2. ogdo		but what is (2)_____.
		(3)_____ who does what is
A3. oaeynn		(2)_____ is from God.
		(3)_____ who does what
A4. ogd		is evil has not seen (4)_____.

B1. ciks		Heal the (1)_____, raise the dead, cleanse those who have
B2. rolyeps		(2) _____, drive out
B3. nedmos		(3) _____.
B4. devirece		Freely you have (4) _____,

C1. sewi		Be (1) _____ about what is
C2. odgo		(2), _____ and
C3. tencinno		(3) _____ about what is evil.

(A) 3 John 1:11; (B) (Matthew 10:8; (C) Romans 16:19

Sons of Jacob Ladder

We are Jacob's sons. Can you name us?
Look us up in Genesis 29:31-30:22 and 35:22-26 if you need help.
Each blank represents one letter.

1. I was my father's favorite son, yet became a slave in Egypt. **J** _ _ _ _ _

2. I am the first son of Zilpah. _ **A** _

3. My name sounds like the Hebrew word for "reward." _ _ _ _ **C** _ _ _

4. I am the next to the oldest son. _ _ _ _ **O** _

5. I am the last son born to Leah. _ _ **B** _ _ _ _

6. I am the eighth son. _ **S** _ _ _

7. I am son number six. _ _ _ _ _ **L** _

8. I am Rachel's second son. _ _ _ _ **A** _ _ _

9. A kingdom bore my name. _ _ **D** _ _

0. I am the first son of Bilhan. **D** _ _

1. My family served in the temple. _ **E** _ _

2. I am Jacob's oldest son. **R** _ _ _ _

Still More Quote Anagrams

Complete each Bible verse by first unscrambling the numbered words and writing them in the second column. Then write the words on the corresponding, numbered blanks.

A1. deeprci		He was (1)_____ for our transgressions, he was
A2. hursced		(2) _____ for our iniquities; the punishment that brought us
A3. aceep		(3)_____ was upon him,
A4. downsu		and by his (4) _____
A5. deelah		we are (5) _____.

B1. dismow		(1)_____ is better than
B2. snowpea		(2)_____ of war, but one
B3. rinesn		(3) _____ destroys much good.

C1. mean		A good (1) _____ is more
C2. sirche		desirable than great (2) _____;
C3. meetsdee		to be (3) _____ is better than
C4. livers		(4) _____ or gold.

(A) Isaiah 53:5; (B) Ecclesiastes. 9:18; (C) Proverbs 22:1

Triumphal Entry

Choose the correct ending to each statement.
If you need help, see Mark 11:1-11.

1. Jesus sent two disciples to find
    A. a colt.　　　B. a room.　　　C. a water pot.

2. The men found one tied at a
    A. stable.　　　B. well.　　　C. doorway.

3. No one had ever
    A. ridden it.　　　B. bought it.　　　C. lost it.

4. The disciples threw their
    A. arms　　　B. cloaks　　　C. ropes

5. over it before Jesus
    A. sat on it.　　　B. walked it.　　　C. touched it.

6. Some people spread their
    A. mats　　　B. sandals　　　C. cloaks

7. out on the
    A. rooftops　　　B. road　　　C. field

8. and others spread out
    A. seeds.　　　B. straw.　　　C. branches.

9. "Hosanna!" The people in front and behind
    A. wept.　　　B. shouted.　　　C. howled.

10. Jesus rode on into
    A. Jerusalem.　　　B. a stable.　　　C. Simon's house.

True or False?

1. Isaac refused to go with Abraham to Mt. Moriah to make a sacrifice.   T   F

2. Three times one night Paul denied knowing Christ.   T   F

3. God created birds on the fifth day.   T   F

4. John was exiled to the island of Patmos.   T   F

5. Jesus walked on the calm waters of Galilee.   T   F

6. A wife of noble character is a diligent worker.   T   F

7 . God is slow to anger and abounding in love.   T   F

8. On the day of Christ's Resurrection, the disciples were afraid of the Jews.   T   F

9. Jesus paid a tax with a coin taken from a fish's belly.   T   F

10. Gamaliel placed Christ' s body in a new tomb.   T   F

11. Zacchaeus welcomed Jesus into his home gladly.   T   F

12. After a day on Mount Carmel, Elisha got caught in the rain.   T   F

(1) Genesis 22: 2-3; (2) Mark 14:66-72 (3) Genesis 1:20-23; (4) Revelation 1:9 (5) John 6:18-19; (6) Proverbs 31:10-31; (7) Psalm 86 :15; (8) John 20:19; (9) Matthew 17:24, 27; (10) Luke 23: 50-53; (11) Luke 19: 6; (12) 1 Kings 18: 45

Twelves

1. According to Luke, Satan entered one of the twelve apostles. Name him. _____

2. Whose throne had twelve lions standing on the six steps? _____

3. King Nebuchadnezzar dreamed about an enormous tree. Twelve months later, as he was boasting, what happened to him? _____

4. Who found Elisha plowing with twelve yoke of oxen and threw his cloak around him? _____

5. Why were the people astonished when Jairus' twelve-year-old daughter got up and walked? _____

6. What city has the names of the twelve apostles written on its twelve foundations? _____

7. In that city, where are the names of the twelve tribes of Israel written? _____

8. How often will the tree of life in the new Jerusalem bear fruit? _____

9. What was left over after Jesus fed more than 5000 people with one boy's lunch? _____

10. Joshua chose twelve men to bring a stone each. What were the stones for? _____

(1) Luke 22:3; (2) 2 Chronicles 9:15-19; (3) Daniel 4:28-34; (4) 1 Kings 19:19; (5) Mark 5:35-42; (6) Revelation 21:10, 14; (7) Revelation 21:12; (8) Revelation 22:2; (9) Matthew 14:20; (10) Joshua 4:3-7

1992, The STANDARD PUBLISHING Company
Permission is granted to reproduce this page for classroom use only—not for resale

Who Would You Rather Be? Why?

Adam or Abraham? _____

Caleb or Cain? _____

David or Daniel? _____

Dorcas or Deborah? _____

Elijah or Eli? _____

Esau or Enoch? _____

Eve or Esther? _____

Goliath or Gideon? _____

Jacob or Joseph? _____

Job or Jonathan? _____

Jonah or Jesse? _____

Joshua or John the Baptist? _____

Mary or Miriam? _____

Peter or Paul? _____

Rhoda or Ruth? _____

Saul or Solomon? _____

Who Are We?

Name the animal and person in each of these Bible stories.

1. I had a man inside me for three days.

2. My rider couldn't see the angel but I could.

3. We delivered food to a man twice a day.

4. I talked a sinless woman into eating something she knew she was not to touch.

5. Jesus said my owner would leave ninety-nine other animals to come look for me.

6. We punished some youths who laughed at this bald prophet of God.

7. When the wonderful teacher rode me into Jerusalem, people spread palm branches on the road.

8. This man wanted to gather the Jews to him like I do my young.

9. As foretold, we got rid of this wicked queen who was pushed out of a window.

10. These parents of a very special baby brought me to the temple for an offering.

) Matthew 12:40; (2) Numbers 22:30-32; (3) 1 Kings 17:2-6; (4)Genesis 3:4-
(5) Luke 15:4; (6) 2 Kings 2:23, 24; (7) Matthew 21:6-8; (8) Matthew 23:1,
; (9) 2 Kings 9:10, 30-35; (10) Luke 2:22-24

Liars

Match the person with the lie he or she told and to the one who heard the lie.

1. "You will not surely die."

2. "She is my sister."

3. "I did not laugh."

4. "I am Esau, your firstborn. I have done as you told me."

5. He gave his older daughter in marriage instead of the younger one.

6. "We found this. Examine it to see whether it is your son's robe."

7. "At dusk…the men left. I don't know which way they went."

8. She put an idol in her husband's bed and said, "He is ill."

9. "Tie me with seven fresh thongs and I'll be as weak as other men."

10. "Yes, that is the price."

Abraham
Jacob
Sarah
Satan
Samson
Michal
Rahab
Sapphira
Laban
Jacob's sons

Eve
God/Abraham
Delilah
Jacob
King's Men
Peter
Jacob
Saul's Men
Pharaoh
Isaac

(1) Genesis 3:4; (2) Genesis 12:10-15; (3) Genesis 18:15; (4) Genesis 27:19; Genesis 29:18-24; (6) Genesis 37:32; (7) Joshua 2:3-5; (8) 1 Samuel 19:12-1 (9) Judges 16:6-10; (10) Acts 5:1-8

© 1992, The STANDARD PUBLISHING Compa
Permission is granted to reproduce this page for classroom use only—not for res

Who Said It?

Match each statement to the person who made it.

1. "O God, please heal her."   David

2. "Take heart, daughter, your faith has healed you."   Elisha

3. "My little daughter is dying. Please come and put your hands on her so that she will be healed and live."   Jacob

4. "Go! It will be done just as you believed it would."   Jairus

5. "You will not surely die."   Jesus

6. "It's been useless—all my watching over this fellow's property in the desert so that nothing of his was missing. He has paid me back evil for good."   Moses

7. "But my brother Esau is a hairy man, and I'm a man with smooth skin."   Rachel

8. "You don't really love me. You've given my people a riddle, but you haven't told me the answer."   Jesus

9. "Give me children, or I'll die!"   Satan

10. "Bring me a new bowl and put salt in it. The Lord says: 'I have healed this water.'"   Samson's wife

(1) Numbers 12:13; (2) Matthew 9:22; (3) Mark 5:22-23; (4) Matthew 8:13; (5) Genesis 3:4; (6) 1 Samuel 25:21; (7) Genesis 27:11; (8) Judges 14:16; (9) Genesis 30:1; (10) 2 Kings 2:19-21

© 1992, The STANDARD PUBLISHING Company
Permission is granted to reproduce this page for classroom use only—not for resale

Who, What, How?

1. Who was Hephzibah's twelve-year-old son who became king? _____
2. Who was Samson's father? _____
3. Who was Samuel's father? _____
4. Who was Samuel's mother? _____
5. Who was the mother of Jesus? _____
6. How did Samson use torches to get even with the Philistines? _____
7. How did Samson use a donkey's jawbone? _____
8. What did Jacob bury under the oak at Shechem? _____
9. During his forty days on Mt. Sinai, how much bread and water did Moses use? _____
10. What did ravens deliver morning and evening to the Kerith Ravine? _____
11. What was Elijah's first request of the widow of Zarephath? _____
12. What is another name for manna? _____
13. What kind of bread does the model wife of Proverbs 31 not eat? _____
14. What did Jesus mean when he warned against the yeast of the Pharisees and Sadducees? _____
15. What reward did Saul offer to the one who killed Goliath? _____

(1) 2 Kings 21:1; (2) Judges 13; (3) 1 Samuel 1:19, 20; (4) 1 Samuel 1:20; (5) Matthew 1:18; (6) Judges 15:3-5; (7) Judges 15:15; (8) Genesis 35:4; (9) Deuteronomy 9:9; (10) 1 Kings 17:6; (11) 1 Kings 17:10-11 (12) Psalm 78:2; (13) Proverbs 31:27; (14) Matthew 16:5-12; (14) 1 Samuel 17:25

Whose Relatives?

Sort the names at the bottom of the page into family groups. Use each name only once. Then tell whether the first-named person (printed) in each set is the oldest.

1. Joseph _____ _____

2. Adam _____ _____

3. Moses _____ _____

4. Noah _____ _____

5. Isaac _____ _____

6. Saul _____ _____

7. Laban _____ _____

8. Solomon _____ _____

9. John the Baptist _____ _____

10. Timothy _____ _____

Relatives: Abel, Abraham, Bathsheba, Benjamin, Cain, David, Elizabeth, Eunice, Ham, Jacob, Jochebed, Jonathan, Leah, Lois, Mary, Mephibosheth, Miriam, Rachel, Sarah, Shem

Decipher the Speaker

Use this key to decipher the name of the person who made each statement.

1. "And who knows but that you have come to royal position for such a time as this?"

2. "May the Lord keep watch between you and me when we are away from each other."

3. "I know that my Redeemer lives, and that in the end he will stand upon the earth."

4. "The Lord is my shepherd, I shall not be in want."

   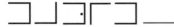

5. "Your people will be my people and your God my God."

6. "I will set out and go back to my father and say to him, Father, I have sinned against heaven and against you."

© 1992, The STANDARD PUBLISHING Company
Permission is granted to reproduce this page for classroom use only—not for resale

7. "I have seen a Philistine woman in Timnah; now get her for me as my wife."

⌋⌊>⌋<◇ _____

8. "My God, my God, why have you forsaken me?"

∨☐⌋⌊ ⌋ _____

9. "How long will you waver between two opinions? If the Lord is God, follow him; but if Baal is God, follow him."

☐<⌈∨⌋⌒ _____

10. "I will go to the king, even though it is against the law. And if I perish, I perish."

☐⌋⌊⌒☐∧ _____

11. "Come now, let us reason together … Though your sins are like scarlet, they shall be as white as snow."

⌊⌒☐ <<∧⌐ _____

12. "Why are you hitting your fellow Hebrew?"

><⌋☐⌋ _____

13. "Who is the Lord, that I should obey Him and let Israel go?"

>⌒⌐⌋∧⌋<⌒ _____

14. "Two young men from the company of the prophets have just come. Please give them a talent of silver and two sets of clothing."

⌐☐⌒⌋⌒⌈ _____

Quizzle Answers

Adam and Eve, p. 5: 1-garden 2-tree of knowledge of good and evil 3-man (Adam) 4-asleep 5-shame 6-dust 7-Adam's rib 8-Eve 9-Eve 10-cherubim and flaming sword 11-sixth 12-Cain, Abel, Seth

What Animal Am I? p. 6: 1-two bears 2-a huge fish 3-gold calf 4-viper or snake 5- goat 6-ants 7-lions 8-pigs 9-donkey 10-ravens 11-fox

Beasts Unique, p. 7: 1-elephant 2-blue whale 3-chameleon 4-giant tortoise 5-hummingbird 6-platypus 7-ostrich 8-centipede 9-horse 10-giraffe

Believe It or Not! p. 8: 1-widow of Nain 2-Bartimaeus 3-madman of Gerasene (Gadara) 4-Lazarus 5-woman bleeding 6-Jairus' daughter 7-leper 8-Paul 9-Jesus 10-Elijah

Which Bible Woman Am I? p. 9: 1-Sarah 2-Mary 3-Zipporah 4-Dorcas 5-Orpah 6-Rahab 7-Bathsheba 8-Esther (Hadassah) 9-Rebekah 10-Jezebel 11-Eunice, Lois 12-Elizabeth

Bible People Ladder, p. 11: 1-Job 2-Isaiah 3-Obadiah 4-Luke 5-Ezekiel 6-Peter 7-Daniel 8-John 9-Philemon 10-Joel 11-Esther

Bible Firsts, p. 12: 1-Saul 2-water to wine 3-Cornelius 4-Genesis 5-Esther 6-Stephen 7-"In the beginning God" 8-Barnabas and Saul (Paul) 9-sower and seed 10-"Blessed are the poor in spirit, for theirs is the kingdom of heaven." 11-water turned to blood 12-Simon Peter and Andrew 13-Samson 14-"The Lord is my shepherd, I shall lack nothing." 15-Matthew 16-Nimrod 17-green 18-the angel's flaming sword guarding the way to the tree of life 19-"Pray for those who persecute you." 20-Noah

Baby Moses Mix-up, p. 13: 2, 4, 1, 5, 3.

Baby Jesus Mix-Up, p. 13: 4, 3, 1, 5, 2.

Books: Old or New? p. 14: 1-OT 2-NT 3-NT 4-OT 5-NT 6-OT 7-OT 8-NT 9-OT 10-NT 11-OT 12-OT 13-NT 14-NT 15-NT 16-NT

Come-On-In, p. 15: I am the gate; whoever enters through me will be saved. He will come in and go out, and find pasture. John 10:9

Counsel CryptoQuote, p. 15: Do what is right and good in the Lord's sight, so that it may go well with you. Deuteronomy 6:18

Double Trouble, p. 16: 1-Abraham and Isaac 2-Jacob and Esau 3-David and Goliath 4-David and Jonathan 5-Ananias and Sapphira 6-Cain and Abel 7-Jesus and John the Baptist 8-Joseph and Mary 9-Mary and Martha 10-Adam and Eve

Faith Category, p. 17: Varied answers may include: Finch, finger, fear. Auk, arm ark. Ibis, intestine, innkeeper. Turkey, tooth, tribe. Hawk, heart, heaven.

Fire Category, p. 17: Varied answers may include: Flood, frogs, finger. Inspiration, idol, index finger. Resurrection, rainbow, robin. Exodus, ear, eye

A Family Ladder, p. 18: 1-Zipporah 2-Naamah 3-Esther 4-Rachel 5-Rebekah 6-Felix 7-Anna 8-Miriam 9-Michal 10-Leah 11-Mary

What Food Am I? p. 19: 1-pressed figs 2-red stew (lentil) 3-grapes 4-honey 5-cucumbers, melons, leeks, onions, garlic 6-crumbs 7-olives 8-wine 9-manna 10-five barley loaves and two fish

From the Heart, p. 20: I will praise you, O Lord, with all my heart; I will tell of all your wonders. Psalm 9:1

Isaiah's Praise, p. 20: O Lord, you are my God; I will exalt you and praise your name, for in perfect faithfulness you have done marvelous things, things planned long ago. Isaiah 25:1

Genesis Firsts, p. 21: 1-"You will not surely die." 2-Cain 3-"Cursed a you" 4-sewed-together fig leaves 5-Adam's rib removed 6-Noah 7-flood 8-Ishmael 9-Enoch 10-fruits of the soil and meat 11-"Be fruitful and multiply." 12-Abimilech, learned that Sarah was Abraham's wife 13-Esau and Jacob 14-Reuben 15-eating the forbidden fruit 16-Cain 17-Enoch 18-Adam and Eve 19-animal(s) killed for clothing 20-Garden of Eden

How Many? p. 22: 1-12; 2-120; 3-12; 4-969; 5-11; 6-2; 7-8; 8-9 plus; 9-450 feet long, 75 feet wide; 10-3; 11-600; 12-40; 13-3, Mary Magdalene, Mary the mother of James, and Salome; 14-10; 15-5, 3 brothers and 2 sisters 17-30

Jairus' Story, p. 23: 1 c 2 a 3 b 4 a 5 b 6 c 7 a 8 c 9 a 10 b 11 c

The Master Healer, p. 24: 1-dead 2-pain 3-leprosy 4-fever 5-paralytics 6-possessed 7-deaf 8-sick

Mercy Category, p. 25: Varied answers may include: mica, moose, macaroni, emerald, ermine, egg omelet, ruby, rooster, rye bread, coal, cow, corn bread, yttrium, yearling, yams.

Child Category, p. 25: Varied answers may include: chin, Cleophas, carrot stick, hair, Hezekiah, hot dog, insides, Isaac, ice cream cone, lips, Lazarus, lemon drops, dimple, David, doughnut.

Middle Verse, p. 26: It is better to take refuge in the Lord than to trust a man. Psalm 118:8

How Far? p. 26: As far as the east is from the west, so far has he removed our transgressions from us. Psalm 103:12

Women: Old or New? p. 27: (How each woman is identified may vary.) 1-OT; gave food to David 2-NT; blessed the Christ child 3-OT prophetess 4-NT; raised from dead 5-NT; John the Baptist's mother 6-OT queen 7-NT dealer in purple cloth 8-NT; opened home to Jesus 9-NT; follower of Jesus 10-OT; Moses' sister 11-OT; Ruth's mother-in-law 12-OT; hid spies 13-OT; Moabitess who married Boaz 14-NT; bought spices to anoint Christ's body 15-NT; lied and died 16-OT; Moses' wife

Naaman's Problem, p. 28: 1 b, 2 c, 3 a, 4 b, 5 c, 6 b, 7 c, 8 c, 9 b, 10 a, 11 a.

Men: Old or New? p. 29: (How each man is identified may vary.)1-OT; Adam's son 2-OT; David's son 3-NT; Judean king 4-OT; walked with God 5-NT; fell from a window 6-NT; daughter was sick 7-OT; Saul's son 8-OT; richly ornamented robe 9-OT; king at age eight 10-NT; betrayed Christ 11-NT; lived in Bethny 12-OT; crippled 13-NT; Roman governor 14-NT; short man

Older or Younger? p. 30: 1-Cain, the first baby born 2-Joseph; Rachel's first 3-Elijah, who served first 4-Goliath, the man 5-Absalom, birth is listed first 6-John the Baptist by six months 7-Abraham, the patriarch 8-Moses, who served first 9-Adam, the first created 10-Abraham, by ten years 11-Leah, the older sister 12-Jochebed, the mother 13-Naomi, the mother-in-law 14-Saul, the father 15-Jesse, the father 16-Zechariah, the father 17-Hannah, the mother 18-Enoch, the father 19-Aaron, by three years

Patience Pays, p. 31: Better a patient man than a warrior, a man who controls his temper than one who takes a city. Proverbs 16:32

A Sure Guard, p. 31: He will command his angels concerning you to guard you in all your ways. Psalm 91:11

Quote Anagrams, p. 32: A1-imitate; A2-good; A3-anyone; A4-God B1-sick; B2-leprosy; B3-demons; B4-received. C1-wise; C2-good; C3-innocent

Sons of Jacob Ladder, p. 33: 1-Joseph, 2-Gad, 3-Issachar, 4-Simeon, 5-Zebulun, 6-Asher, 7-Napthtali, 8-Benjamin, 9-Judah, 10-Dan, 11-Levi, 12-Reuben

Still More Quote Anagrams, p. 34: A1-pierced; A2-crushed; A3-peace; A4-wounds; A5-healed. B1-wisdom; B2-weapons; B3-sinner. C1-name; C2-riches; C3-esteemed; C4-silver.
Triumphal Entry, p 35: 1 a, 2 c, 3 a, 4 b, 5 a, 6 c, 7 b, 8 c, 9 b, 10 a
True or False? p. 36: 1 F, 2 T, 3 T, 4 T, 5 F, 6 T, 7 T, 8 T, 9 F (it was from the fish's mouth), 10 F (it was Joseph of Arimathea), 11 T, 12 T
Twelves, p. 37: 1-Judas Iscariot 2-Solomon's 3-He went crazy and lived like an animal for seven years 4-Elijah 5-Because she had been dead. 6 Jerusalem, the Holy City 7-on the gates 8-every month 9-12 baskets full of pieces 10-They were to be a memorial to the fact that the Israelites had crossed Jordan on dry ground.
Who Would You Rather Be? p. 38: Answers will vary.
Who Are We? p. 39: 1-huge fish, Jonah 2-donkey, Balaam 3-ravens Elijah 4-serpent, Eve 5-sheep, good shepherd 6-bears, Elisha 7-colt, Jesus 8-hen, Jesus 9-dogs, Jezebel 10-2 doves or pigeons, Joseph and Mary
Liars, p. 40: 1. Satan (to Eve) 2. Abraham (to Pharaoh) 3. Sarah (to God or to Abraham) 4. Jacob (to Isaac) 5. Laban (to Jacob) 6. Jacob's sons (to Jacob) 7. Rahab (to the king's men) 8. Michal (to Saul's men) 9. Samson (to Delilah) 10. Sapphira (to Peter)
Who Said It? p. 41: 1-Moses 2-Jesus 3-Jairus 4-Jesus 5-serpent (Satan) 6-David 7-Jacob 8-Samson's wife 9-Rachel 10-Elisha
Who, What, How? p. 42: 1-Manasseh 2-Manoah 3-Elkanah 4-Hanna 5-Mary 6-turned tied-together foxes loose with flaming torches to burn the grain fields, vineyards, and olive groves 7-to kill 1000 men 8-foreign god and earrings gathered from his household and entourage 9-none 10—bread and meat 11-water 12-bread of angels 13-bread of idleness 14-to guard against their teaching 15-great wealth, his daughter and tax exemptions
Whose Relatives? p. 43: 1-Benjamin, Jacob, no 2-Abel, Cain, yes ; Jochebed, Miriam, no 4-Ham, Shem, yes 5-Abraham, Sarah, no 6-Jonathan Mephibosheth, yes 7-Rachel, Leah, yes 8-Bathsheba, David, no 9-Elizabeth Mary, no 10-Lois, Eunice, no.
Decipher the Speaker, p. 44: 1-Mordecai (Esther 4:14) 2-Laban (Genesis 31:49) 3-Job (Job 19:25) 4-David (Psalm 23:1) 5-Ruth (Ruth 1:1) 6-Prodigal son (Luke 15:18) 7-Samson (Judges 14:2) 8-Jesus (Matthew 27:46) 9-Elijah (1 Kings 18:21) 10-Esther (Esther 4:16) 11-The Lord (Isaiah 1:18) 12-Moses (Exodus 2:13) 13-Pharaoh (Exodus 5:2) 14-Gehazi (2 Kings 5:22).